Poetry From The Nearest Barstool

Paul Tristram

For those who like to point their fucking fingers!

Some of these poems first appeared in *Dead Snakes,
The Camel Saloon, BoySlut, Horror Sleaze Trash,
Literary Orphans, Decanto, The Bactrian Room,
Poeticdiversity: The Litzine Of Los Angeles,
Thirteen Myna Birds, Poetry Salzburg Review,
48th Street Press Broadside Series, Poems-For-All,
The Gambler, Danse Macabre Du Jour, Imaginalis,
Mad Swirl, Poppy Road Review, Pyrokinection,
and Pink Litter.*

Table Of Contents

An Ode To Nothing

When the fear and pain
have fallen away.
Passions both good and bad
have extinguished themselves.
Hunger and thirst are sated.
Memories and experience dismissed.
The core,
hollow and still
and quiet
without yearning.
When want is unwanted.
Truth irrelevant.
Climate merely background.
And true seeing
involves more than just
the eyes.
There
you will find me.
Whispering
my ode to nothing.

The Ballad Of A Broken Man

With a heavy heart
in splinters.
A soul which feels
like mercury drops
falling daily into a drain.
A park bench damaged back.
A left knee he's always
losing an argument with.
A mind that fractured
on that cold full mooned night
all of those years ago
and stayed desolate,
demented and dislocated.
With no more tears left
in his humble possession
they left along time ago
hand in hand with warmth.
A face bruised,
burnt and scarred
but with eyes alive
like I have never seen before.
Crazy, wild and brilliant
like the swirls in the sky
of a Van Gogh painting.
I shudder in respect
as he raises his fists
Heavenward
and once more
squares up
like a prize-fighter
to his aching fate.
I realize that Broken
and Beaten are two
completely different worlds.

She Undid Her Buttons

She undid her buttons
and slid back down the bed…smiling.
I threw my cigarette at the ashtray,
I would deal with the burn marks later
on both carpet and soul.
Tingling with tenderness
I felt lace and magic and everything.
It swirled around my fingers and mind
blowing up into mental fireworks.
Centuries old scars
healed with slight caresses
…reciprocal, reciprocal, reciprocal…
Inside out, Off guard and Scent driven.
I dove from the tip of her chin
to bounce from bellybutton
down into her explosion.
With a rage like passion,
extinguished never.

Another Scream From Block Six

A freezing shiver ran down my spine
as I heard it split open the sky
at first like a hawk in pain
then finally slithering through a moan
and out into a pitiful gurgle.
Such Misery and Wretchedness
screeching from that Tortured Soul,
the Agony of Spirit perfected in Sound.

"Poor John!" I thought out loud.
"Where are the Angels for you?"

Then shaking my frowning head
I resumed my rambling walk
around the Victorian red brick walls
on a damp, misty evening
up on this remote Berkshire hill.

Thieves Will Be Prostituted

I had not seen him for a couple of years,
I had heard the rumours and they looked true.
He had lost a few stone in weight,
his face skin was gaunt and grey,
teeth missing or now just black stubs.
He was sitting on a fold-up chair
with a clipboard and pencil
wearing the florescent waistcoat
of a criminal serving his sentence
outside in the community.
He was a really talented guitarist once
but now he's into sucking heroin's cock again
and sat on a picnic chair outside of a public
toilet like a pervert.

He spotted me passing and scrounged a roll-up

"What's up mate, how are you?"

"Hey, the Man got me ticking how many slag's
go into the 'Ladies' and how many assholes
go into the 'Gents' I've gotta record it all down,
a little tick for each and every one!"

"Shit, why do they need to know that?
It's a free service when you're not in London,
they're not checking on customers like!"

"I know but the Man's got to find me something
to do for 3 hours a week, innit!"

I wished him luck and walked off,
it was nice to witness a messed-up scenario
that I wasn't actually involved in, for once!

The Widow's Scar

Throbbed and ached on occasion
like a snake of memory
from her once married bedroom life,
which for years now
she had wrestled nemesistically
and unsuccessfully into forgetfulness.
It fascinated the thoughtful
mercurial depths of the long
Edwardian standing mirror.
Played carefully and roughly
with greying, disillusioned fingertips.
Silently hissed out its longing and agonies
when plunged and choked in bathwater.
This Widow's Scar,
the eye socket and teeth of her soul,
devoured Christenings, Weddings,
shadows of yesterday and rosary beads
spitting them back out as curses
and dried up chicken bone knuckles.

Taxidermy Bride

In the cobwebbed shadows
of his long hallway
he sat nervously waiting
upon the partially broken
bottom 3rd stair step.
A whistling excitement
stirred up the dusty leaves
of his delicate, ornate mind.
As he peered downwards
at the Taxidermist's card
beheld betwixt
his porcelain slender fingers.
And read quietly to himself
'your parcel will be
delivered both promptly
and exactly at one and a half
minutes after 6 o'clock
of the evening'
He gulped down wonder
and smiled deeply
with his eyes only.
As the Grandfather clock
not quite 4ft away
struck the 6th hour
and he heard the grind
and clatter of his garden gate
yawning open in the distance.
He rose, shakily
and walked towards
the front door,
each footfall a step further
away from Bachelor.

Splitting Matches

I learnt to do it in Swansea Prison's
Young Offenders Unit,
you could turn a match
into 2 and sometimes 3 lights.
You'd put a single matchstick
down upon the table
get a biro pen
and place the tip just at the base
of the match head.
Then BANG! the top of the pen
with your free palm.
I became quite an expert at it
until I smuggled in a flint stem
from a plastic Clipper lighter.
Built a little box out of matches
slightly smaller than a matchbox
with 2 round tunnels running through it.
I put the flint stem in one
and in the other I had
a string of braided mop head.
I would strike the flint wheel
and the sparks would ignite
the end of the braided mop head
causing it to singe and smoulder ember
and I would light my roll-ups off that.
Nowadays you get a disposable lighter
in your Prison Settling-In Pack
but back in the day that's how we did it.
Besides, when you're only making pence
for cutting straps or making grey mailbags
every little corner you cut helps.

F-Ward (Here We Come!)

On the verge of another breakdown,
suicidal to the very bone
she takes another shot
of gin and misery.
And screams perfectly
inside her head
as her soul falls backwards
in upon itself.
And the squirming starts
again its movement
and rhythm of anger.
The clawing inside her
brain and face
makes her fidget and jump
like a bag of drowning rats.
She tries to focus
and concentrate
upon the curse that is circling her
but again
she ends up too dizzy.
Collapsing from exhaustion
her mind ledge-leaps
into sleep
which is the safest place
for her at the moment.

Oblivionville (The Next Phase)

They'd jammed a chair against the kitchen door handle.
I kicked it open and the skinny, junkie guy ran out
carrying with him his little bag of tricks and misery.
I saw her first track mark on the back of her left hand
I shook my head disappointedly and asked why?
"This is Oblivionville, the next phase and you're either
coming along for the ride with me or you're not?"
I grabbed my cider flagon and denim jacket and left.
20 years later, I heard she threw herself under a train,
she didn't die, one of her legs was hit the wrong way
around and one of her arse cheeks needed to be removed.
We used to be schoolyard sweethearts, once upon a time.
I remember her bringing me bread & butter in the shed
at the bottom of her grandmothers garden where I was
hungry and hiding, she also brought a potted flower
and put it on a shelf by the window to make it look nice.

The Solitude Of The Silversmith

He strains away diligently
by candle and moonlight
in the cobwebbed quietude
of his attic workroom.
Back arched and spectacle nosed
the stamina of an army
expertly directed upon
a single point of focus.
Tiny slivers of moonbeams
confetti fell upon his bench
twist, spiral, spin and dance
as breathing changes pitch.
The backbone breaking posture
of the will targeted upon itself.
The fight between
the artist and ones craft.
The agony and ecstasy
as each brush stroke of the file
paints a picture perfect
striding another high to climb.
The tunnel-visioned stamina
with unique flourish intertwined
is why this master craftsman
remains also a pupil
for he is still learning all the time.

And Wanted All Of It

She lurched forward on crooked knees
with a bent umbrella above her right shoulder.
She smiled through the sky's teardrops
and walked faster, more focused
upon the point of the day
which was him, completely.
She'd ironed his work clothes the night before,
shared a loaf of bread with him,
tangoed imaginatively through his fingers,
kissed the edges of his soul
and wanted all of it.

Violence To Silence

As I walked down the Midnight Avenue
there was a smashing noise from a house
just up ahead on my side of the road.
I looked up in the direction to see
a frying pan whirring through the night time air
and crash into the side window of a parked car.
As I approached I could see that the car window
had completely shattered and the frying pan
was lodged in the middle with the handle sticking
back out onto the pavement like an insane lever.
'Curious and Curiouser' I thought out aloud
as the screaming, off to my left started in earnest.
A door crashed open and a man ran out into the garden
screaming "She's fucking scalded me, Help!"
She came running from around the side of the house
and threw a spinning kettle which hit him
square in the middle of the lower back,
sending him howling painfully down onto his knees.
"What are you fucking looking at, Fuck-face?"
She shrieked, pointing a rigid finger like a gun
with a perfect aim over in my direction.
Lights were flickering on in windows all around
as I carried on down the Avenue, chuckling to myself
and sucking on my Mad Dog 20/20 wine bottle.
I could still hear them fighting back in the garden
behind me but I could only make out animal noises,
some banshee screaming and swear words.
As I reached the end of the Midnight Avenue
and put the key into the outside door of my new bedsit,
a police car drifted silently and slowly up the road.
From the safety of my room I phoned my girlfriend
and told her all about the affray going on outside.
"Oh my god, you'll never get any writing done there,
you need lots of peace and quiet, baby!" she said.

"That's where you're wrong!" I replied with humour
"This is a good start, but I will speak to you later,
for the typewriter's calling me on home once again!"

Battle-Fed

Chaos and Carnage
Rained down like Confetti
the first time I picked up
the Battle Axe.
A Whistling Tornado
inside my Aching Head
torturing Mercy.
Angry Blood
pumping through
my Pitiless Heart.
My Murderous Eyes
view everything
before me
in Butcher's Sections.
Your Cries and Anguish
are perfect Kindling
for the Demon's Fire
that is Forever
Raping my Soul.
It has Always been this Way
and it Will always be this Way!
We are all merely
Links of Chain
in this Daily War of Life.
I am Simply Catching my Breath.
Surveying the Arena
both left and right.
Mopping my Hating Brow
with your Stuttering Fear.
Before once more
Releasing my Roar!

A Haberdashery Of Heartache

He stepped quickly in through
the gloomy, creaking shop front door,
leaving the drizzly rain of London's
'Bleeding Heart Yard' behind him.
Removing his battered old trilby hat
he shook it casting little sooty globs
of water down onto the sawdust floor.
He approached the teeth marked counter
and rang the little bronze bell, thrice.
An assistant quickly appeared from behind
a dusty velvet curtained doorway
wearing an apron which was splattered
with blood to the extent that he could have
previously been employed as sidekick
to Him who tore up Lady Elizabeth Hatton.
He adjusted the small round spectacles
upon his long and crooked nose,
scratched at his balding head
whilst pulling a pencil nubbing out
from behind his greasy right ear
(such as the kind you find in a gambling den!)
He tapped the lead against his tongue, twice,
coughed and spoke thus,
"Is the slash & stitching for yourself, sir?
How long was this previous relationship, in years?
Was a wedding band used to bind the contract?
Is the enemy still alive and well or deceased?
Ankle-biters, are there any ankle-biters, sir?
If so how many of them and of what sex
also, is there any fondness for any of them
or are they merely relationship baggage?
Please, don't look that way, sir, I must ask.
Last but not least, the guilt, there is always guilt,
on this occasion which side of the fence does it lay?"

The patron winced and shuffled uncomfortably
from one foot back and fore to the other,
then spoke his reply in an exhausted drawl
"It would have been thirteen years to this day.
Yes, the messy business is for myself.
There was a brass contractual finger ring
but I spied it in a 'Leaving Shop' window
3 streets ago only yesterday morning.
God, did not bless the coupling with children,
but with enough misery to fill the hole instead.
And as for the guilt, well while I do not
have a decent thing to say about her
being a gentleman, I must take responsibility
for letting her into my home to begin with!"
The assistant finished noting this down
and with a frown he spoke again,
"You must not be too hard on yourself,
it speaks for itself that you are stood here
and she is not, sir!
Besides we are not here to judge but to mend
Repairing butchered hearts is our business
and our business is very well and healthy.
It will be a whole 3 banknotes for the operation,
which will take approximately one single hour.
It is indeed your lucky day, sir.
This morning's work ran rather smoothly,
the first after midday vitals didn't make it though,
hence the state of my normally spotless apparel.
The lady who was supposed to be up next
and booked her appointed yesterday afternoon
could not wait the 24 hours or so
for we have just been informed that she took
a permanent dip off Shadwell Docks last night.
Which gives us a 2 hour gap until the next one.
The Master is out back smoking his pipe,
if you take a seat, I will give him a shout

and we will both be with you directly, sir!"

The Welsh Drover

Following the arseholes
of the animals in front
for two days more.
Feet, ankle deep
in English shit and mud.
Through to Market Day
with all the necessary nonsense
and kack which pockmarks it.
Then finally with paper
stamped and scribbled,
pockets brimming a-chinkle.
Turning fast upon heel,
heading mountain-ward again
where the road home
changes level
like a lovers curving breast
with each new step taken.
And the trees, my God the trees
which cannot be described
with any form of justice
to anyone but Welsh-folk.
That fresh Glamorganshire
dawn slapping red and friendly
your healthy cheeks like a
grandmother who's missed you
from the bottom of her heart.
Then at last your Village
opens up before you
with that deep aching bend
as familiar as the tilting slope
along the inside
of your married elbow.
Until it banks gently…that way
to your little house

where she lays asleep
misting the little back upstairs
window with her presence,
as warm as Mayday,
fried cockles and bacon
awaiting your most blessed return.

`

Poaching Lovers

It is the only thing that makes him smile
especially since his reflection's started to age.
Yet, it is all just a cruel front.
The meanness is as real as dogshit
but the coolness he once owned
has began fading and become instead
a coldness which has seeped into his bones
and spirits and left him helpless when alone,
to rock himself neurotically asleep
with heavy heart and glistening cheek.
The SCARS they CARVED
into his vulnerable childhood mind
SHINE in NEON
when everyone else's backs are turned.
Which, in turn, makes him crumble,
pitifully down onto his desperate knees.
Unless of course, he has used his 'trick'
found someone new and naïve to prey upon,
lie too and destroy slowly, piece by piece.
For then he has someone else's ROT
to focus on and temporarily replace
the massive burden of his OWN repulsive soul.

Arrogance Is Such A Slippery Slope…But I Like It!

"Arrogance is such a slippery slope…but I like it!"
he muttered in a melodically low half-whisper.
Whilst staring carefully into a large wall-hanging
'Absinthe' advertisement barroom mirror
and polishing his Anarchy Symbol engraved
silver upper left lateral incisor, delicately
with the corner of a burgundy and black paisley cravat.
Then spinning his debauched, battered Victorian top hat
up from barstool top and onto his half-drunken head,
replacing brass knuckles and both mother of pearl
pillboxes into waistcoat pockets, he slips on his ebony
crushed velvet tailcoat and smiling a sweet 'Nos Da'
to the other patrons of this dilapidated drinking house
with a sweep of his right hand he flips the solid steel rod
walking cane from floor to underarm he strode on out
through the tavern door which one of the street corner
girls in his company was sleazily holding a-jar for him.
After 4 or 5 minutes of silence a bald, beer bellied
middle-aged man tentatively glanced around and spoke.
"Jesus Christ, that Guy gives me the willies, can we
have the football on the box now, Shadwell are playing?
I would have said something earlier only I was here
the very last time he brought his knives out of hiding!"

She's Burnt Her Hair Again

All up the left-hand side of her head
and she rocks jerkily back and forth
in a mechanical mid-speed rhythm.
Dribbling chalky medication tasting spittle
carefully out of the corner of her mouth
to drop between her bare-self-harmed-knees
to add to the gob butterfly she is making
upon the grey square linoleum tile
down between her swollen, dangerous feet.
There is a Guard sat bored 4ft away
daydreaming of normal things
and wishing to be somewhere else.
It takes stamina, tenacity, patience and practice
to get the rocking motion perfect.
If she changes pitch or frequency even slightly
a cog might slip, a wheel derail
and The Fracture which dwells inside her forehead
will open up again and swallow whole
a big bunch of her 'Happy Ever After's'

The Smudge Trick

I saw them both approaching through the crowd
and separate just up ahead then slide back in towards
their Target, which on this occasion was Me.
The one on my right lifted his lit cigarette up to his
mouth a split second before the orchestrated collision.
I stepped forward and twisted, slamming his cigarette
back into his face with my shoulder whilst grabbing
the wrist tightly of the one upon my left who was
reaching for my jacket pocket and bent it back sharply.
Both of them yelped just like little scolded puppy dogs.
I stopped and glared at both of them in silence for a
second or two until they both disappeared backwards
in different directions into the fast moving crowd.
The object of the con is: to get cigarette ash upon
your shoulder as an excuse to make physical contact
so they can apologise profusely for their own silly
clumsiness whilst innocently dusting the ash off you.
All the time that this is going on the one stationed
at the other side of you is making the pocket dip,
it's called 'The Smudge Trick' and like everything
else in life choosing the wrong target can be painful.

Thirsty For A Hangover

I skedaddled with a swagger through the town
with my eyes and paintbrush as bloody red
as freshly inflicted emotional stab wounds.
I did the pubs and clubs from right to left,
then left to right and back again once more,
leaving friends, acquaintances and enemies
dropping like sizzling flies in my blurry wake.
I climbed a rooftop avoiding queues, trampled
strangers underfoot and ate something not very
pleasant and greasy whilst I was still running.
I lost a coat but found myself a much better one,
avoided the Police with an almost second sense,
slid around and through Bouncers without even
slightly colliding, bribing, cajoling or arguing.
Broke up a fist fight then started two or three,
sniffed her popper bottle as I slithered passed,
bought some take-outs and a rather handsome
'Peaky Blinders' flat cap off a subway busker.
Walked over to the river finally slowing down,
threw in my last pound coin and made a wish,
sat upon the bank drinking the bottle dregs,
smiling widely and waiting for her approach.

Under The Patchwork Cloudscape Of Future Childhood Memories

Upon the grass of Victoria Gardens
my Father and his Associates would lounge
drinking Strongbow cider
and Old England Medium Sherry
straight from the bottle necks.
I can still hear them now,
people don't drink like that anymore,
the sound was amazing
like a starving man eating a piece
of their favourite food, loudly.
Each man was having a liquid banquet
all by themselves.
As I sat there only 8 or 9 years old,
chewing on a hock bone
from the butchers in Neath Market.
Under the patchwork cloudscape
of future childhood memories
listening to them talk of Valium,
Ativan, Speed and Soap Bar,
of different prisons and how they're changing.
Which Policemen were Bastards
and which ones were fair and alright.
Then after the stories they'd trade scars
always trying to outdo each other,
stab wounds and razor slashes,
broken bottle and pint glass circles,
dog attacks and crossbow bolts.
They'd hold up their drunken hands
and count out loud the broken fingers
then bow down their heads to show
the small angry red horseshoe shaped
truncheon wounds that were never stitched
but left to horribly heal by themselves.

I remember a few years later
2 young loser boys from our street
came and got me because my 'Old Man'
had got his hand through the wooden
slats of a park bench, right up to the wrist
and couldn't get it back out again.
So after I had spent a small eternity
laughing my head off and asking him
how the Hell he had managed to do it?
I boot that wooden slat right out
with my Dr Martens, setting him free
the 'Old Man' used it as a walking staff
for the rest of the day and took it home.
Some children had Disneyland
or days out in Blackpool or Alton Towers
and they are more than welcome to them.
For I would not change a single one of my
patchwork cloudscape childhood memories
spent with 'The Neath Cidernauts.'
for the world and that ain't no lie, Boyo!

Like A Train Ran Over My Soul
And All The Ambulances In The World Blew Up
Applauding It

It had just stopped raining, a few days before Christmas
5:30 in the afternoon, freezing cold and already dark.
I stepped out of the warm pub –where I was waiting
for her to finish up the last bits of festive shopping-
to smoke a small cigar and collect my rambling thoughts.
And there he was, ragged and destitute, sitting in the
doorway of a Property Agents a mere 3ft or so away,
the irony of it was like a big, fat slap in the senses.

"You haven't got a spare light there have you, buddy?"

I handed him my box of 'England's Glory' matches
and when he had finished using 2 of them to light
a dog-end which was no longer than my little fingernail
I told him to keep the box and we started to converse.
He told me that everyone called him Jesus and that he
had been on the road for 6 Winters this coming January.
I asked him what had gone wrong to make that happen?
He merely winced, shrugged his shoulders and replied

"It was just like a train ran over my soul and all the
ambulances in the world blew up applauding it!"

I took out my wallet and handed him a crisp £20 note,
told him not to spend it all on food and then asked
him if there was anything else that I could do for him?

"You've already done more than you can possibly know,
you've given me one free night safe away from the wolves
and that desperate 12 hours is sometimes just enough!"
Then he rose, bowed and swaggered off deeper into town.

Tenterhooks

She is in the corner hotel
upstairs and rushing
from one window to the other
hoping to catch a glimpse of him
coming up the wet Glastonbury street.
He is 5 hours late already
and they would have found her note
by now and know that she has run away.
Her head suspects that something's wrong,
that he's changed his mind?
But her heart will not accept this!
She takes another swig of laudanum
whilst looking at his likeness
imprisoned inside a little wooden locket.
Then she is back to the windows
frantic once more.
And that is where we leave her
hanging upon desperate tenterhooks
as the afternoon dims into evening
waiting alone with her fate.

In The Petrichor Dawn

With the battered feet of a Rover,
heart 'The Fool' card
of the Tarot's Major Arcana,
I bob and weave
along Poacher's trails,
blackberry brambled back lanes
and old disused, rusty railway lines.
Face sobering up nicely
in the early morning light
as I drag my still hung-over shadow
kicking and screaming
behind my sometimes sideways step.
It is the little things which burst
miracles and wonder
inside your adult mind.
The flaking black paint
of a familiar garden gate
after hours of dark stumbling
is almost enough to make you
fall back in love with life again.
A house door that key still fits into
simply underlines and completes
the luck and beautiful magic of it all,
as upstairs creaks alive, gently,
to inform you that she really is still here.

The Girl With Feet Coming Backwards Out Of Her Mouth

She heaved, choking momentarily
then heaved again
an upside down labour of sorts.
All smoky dry and charcoal tasting,
a new flashback appeared
with each new centimetre revealed.
As she coughed and gagged upon
the ghosts and bones of yesterday.
Again, she tried uselessly using hands
but they were no good
except for gripping tight
the burning bars of determination.
It was her Soul pushing contractions,
her Conscience applying midwifery
until finally a snapping sensation
and it all fell away free with a slump.
The Now useless carcass
of naïve innocence curled up
in a butchered un-miracle
before her wiser, resentful, adult eyes.

The Twisted Tower

The Twisted Tower inside
is where they hide from the day.
Chained within cells of grief.
Like onions, layer upon layer
of depression, lust and anger
encase their wretched souls.
There is no light in addiction.
No comfort found in darkly
suckling selfishness and greed.
Violence is not the answer,
It is the root of a problem
which if watered by Impact
spreads within your personality
like snaking, barbed wire brambles.
Lies beget lies and opens up the door
to the rest of falsehoods family.
Meanness makes you unworthy of love
It really is that obvious and simple.
There's a Twisted Tower being built
inside all of us with each hard experience.
Yet, there is another side to that coin,
the beauty of it is that each of us
has our own individual key,
it's all just a matter of finding it
and stepping out into the sunshine.

SlaveMasterSlave

Slight nauseous whiplash
from role reversal.
Climatizing the rack
of deep, disturbing delight.
She spits for lubrication,
tearing gasps
from sensory deprived ghosts
and artistically smudging
trickling and dribbling
bits of this and that.
Back buckled arching
anciently ceiling-ward
in in riotous climatic
stuttering frenzy.
Ball bearing smooth
in shameless infamy.
A sweating leather pit of leisure,
a clicking traction to pain.
The glory of discomfort,
a smarting smack makes tender
everything once again.
A breathing canvas
glistening and aching.
The flow and ebb of tolerance,
The wax and wane of indifference.

Those Drunken Heights Of Absurdity & Glory
In Between Hangovers!

The scars, bumps and lumps.
Fractured, broken, flaked and chipped
teeth and bones.
The tattoos both decorative
and gang related.
The days ticked away
in different prison cells in different prisons.
The countless nights dragged in through
and kicked out of
the 'Wooden-Pillowed Hotel'
revolving police station doors.
Fighting the system, each other
or whoever came along first
both winning and losing loads of times.
Running team-handed down back lanes
well past midnight
escaping the flashing blue light menace.
Nights freezing in skips and bins,
shivering under a thin blanket
of loose cardboard and paper.
The first Roast Dinner and pint of Ruddles Bitter
after a 4 day walk to get home, ah!
Bedding down with deranged, psychotic women
nearly half as crazy as your demented self.
Smiling bravely or sometimes idiotically
through the torrential rain and pain of it all.
Waking up and sharing a flat flagon
with those 2 rigid fingers
that have been sticking up in your face
ever since the hour of your birth.
Insanity, nervous breakdowns, addictions and excess.
The complete fucking derangement and self abandonment
of the mind, body and soul.

34

The punk rock, the adrenalin, the energy and the vice.
Realizing that both losing and winning
are part of life's game and not slowing down
because of either.
I would not change any of it, nor spare the rod once.
For on my deathbed I'll smile because I will know
that I did not waste my life at all,
I experienced it and lived it to the full
and squeezed out every last drop before leaving.

I'm Trying To Find A Stepladder To Get Out Of This!

He kept repeating frantically
to the other confused patients
in the afternoon common room.
Until the sectioned bag-lady
screamed and attacked him
with the bottom of a fruit bowl.
The teenage boy and girl
on suicide watch in the corner
both felt guilty immediately.
The blind retired magistrate
scared to death of loud noises
began crying and pissed his pants.
The school dinner lady with OCD
started to fix and rearrange
the curtains whilst naming all
of the Disciples backwards.
Dancing Edna began discreetly
flashing her lemon panties
and Billy 'False Teeth' started
turning into a werewolf again.
Whilst mean old Tilly 2 Canes
stood by the side of the TV
watching John The Baptist
with anger management issues
who had been for 5 days solid
tenaciously playing 'Donkey Kong'
finally make it to the last level.
And as he stuttered and bounced
excitedly towards the finishing line
she pulled the plug from the wall
and drown him with her screaming.

One Pound Notes

A pocket full of them
and you felt loaded
even though you probably
only had £20 on you.
I remember being on Windsor Road
and walking past a taxi place
there were 3 of us
up to no good, as usual.
We spied an extremely inebriated man
half sitting, half laying
upon a chair in the waiting room.
He had around 30 one pound notes
in his lap, falling off his legs
and on the floor all around his feet.
His woman friend was on her knees
laughing and picking them all up
whilst he was singing loudly
"On the streets where you live!"
In we ran like psychic thieves
not a word had passed our mouths
we each grabbed a single
one pound note from his lap
and ran back out into the street.
'In Like Flynn' and fluid as always,
we didn't need it
and it was only a pound note each,
we could have robbed him blind.
It was for the thrill, the rush of it
the excitement of living.
I miss one pound notes
the pound coins are not the same
although a handful of them
forcefully flung up close, in defence
did save me from being stabbed, one night.

Leopard Print Carpet Burns

I sat opposite her, fascinated!
As she chain-smoked Malboro Red's
whilst pouring us both another
nasty glass of cheap white wine.
Her faded black-eye looked beautiful,
she had in only one hoop earring
which un-symmetricalized
the whole glorious appearance.
Wearing a dull-white vest top
with a lactating stain over the left breast
which was confusing
as I had just been assured
that there were no children in the place?
Then her knees were a work of art, indeed,
one bandaged (Soiled decoratively!)
the other bruised and scabbed up
just like the leopard print
the Punk and Skinhead Girls
would dye their crew-cuts back in the 80's.
I felt my cock squirm and tingle, playfully
as she caught me looking and explained
"Last night was the first week
that me and my girlfriend have ever gone
without fighting, so we celebrated!"
"Cool!" I replied with a merry smile.
"The room will be £80 a week, up front!"
she stated, pulling me back into reality.
"Cool!" I replied again
"I'll take it, when I can move in?"

Disillusionment (Home Sweet Home!)

"Hey, It's so nice to see you again, Sir.
It's been quite a long time, hasn't it?
Anyway, did you have a pleasant trip
out there this time…sorry, stupid question!
Just the 1 bag, you're travelling light.
I'd give you the menu but you never eat
anything for the first few days, do you?
Well, you haven't really missed much here.
Old Nancy died a couple of months ago,
gone up to that big old bar in the sky.
Willy Tinker left yesterday for London,
he's landed himself a job constructing
suicidal manuals for a top publishing house.
But hark at me, rambling on in this way.
You look worn out and exhausted.
We've got your regular room prepared
down on the 'Shadowy Wing' for you.
Here's the key along with 5 free tokens
for the 'Scream Machine'
along with your complimentary bottle
of the Houses own 'Sour Grapes Wine.'
It's good to see you back with us again,
you know your own way down, Sir!"

Give Them Enough Ground And They'll Walk On It

Like moths to a bright flame,
metal filings to a magnet,
they sense that you are different
that you think in a unique way.
Live outside of the box
that most people are born and trapped in.
You do not care for their rules
and opinions and way of life.
For you are too busy inventing
your own as you go along.
They will flock to you,
the women will want to sleep with you,
to marry you , to own you.
The men to be your friend,
your best friend, your important friend
the only friend that matters.
You will listen to them, watchful,
drink with them until it gets stale.
And they will 'turn'
because being with you
will not be enough.
They will hate you
because by being by you
reveals just how shallow and lost
they really are.
Then they will scheme in the shadows
to snuff out the light
which they were once drawn to.
With venom and hatred
because that light is rare,
it's a unique soul
and it shows the soulless
just how miserable and base
in envy, jealousy and bitterness

they really are.
There is no help for their kind
they are the shit beneath your boot
scrape them off and keep walking on.
Let them applaud their own devilment
as you enter into new realms
of destiny and glory.

Sex Slave To Celibacy

So you tell me that you going to try
celibacy for the next 12 months.
To have a break from the games
and the weekend hunting.
Giving your heart and emotions
time to heal and slow down.

Why would you tell me this?
I have an instant hard-on.
I feel it awaken to a semi
then curl up and into a full erection
within a second and a half.
I look down and see it
through my old work jeans
wriggling alive like a purring snake
beneath the worn denim.

Your mouth is too full for celibacy!
Your eyes were made to shine
screaming orgasms through.
I try to think about you not needing sex
ignoring the throbbing, weeping flesh bone
alive and hungry within my lap
and the opposite happens.
I see you awake to a cloud of silky sighs,
pushing the blankets from your bare legs
and your swollen, moist pussy lips
kissing the inside of your panties
softly, delicately, teasingly.

I feel your hair twisted around my fingers
with your head pulled backwards,
your body arched with arse cheeks
splayed wide as I thunder perfectly

like a flesh and bone battering-ram,
peeking to a speed-blur right up behind you.
Spurting with momentum
the volume of my sticky, eager seed
straight into the furnace at your pussy's heart.

Then it switches and you are sucking
the pearly strings of pre-cum
off and around the purple head of my cock.
While I am pushing my tongue rapidly
into the burgundy fleshiness of your cunt,
lapping in and out and around
zigzagging the musky trace between your lips
and drawn like a magnet up to your clit.

Then it changes once more
it is now just a headshot of you, smiling
your warm, friendly smile.
The jerking has ebbed away
the throbbing reduced itself to sensitivity
as I dab away the last glistening traces
and flush!
I wash my hands and call you back
to tell you that celibacy is a big step
that maybe you should give yourself
a little more time to think it over.
But if you would like to discuss it further
I will be available later on this evening?

Tatting

You should see them all on Bin Night
coming down from that Council Estate
up on top of that hill over on Cheap-side.
Into the Town they come scavenging
like marauding packs of rats and hyenas.
Raiding the rubbish bags, wheelie-bins,
skips and refuse piles of respectable folk.
Drunk and singing as they blatantly do it,
with no shame or discretion in their antics.
It's become a barbarous weekly ritual,
I once saw a young couple copulating
upon a neighbours unwanted roadside sofa.
A group of middle-aged women brawling
over a mouldy old pair of velvet curtains
their men laughing and egging them on.
The Police turn up after the fun has begun
to arrest the usual suspects each week
under the 'Stealing By Finding' laws.
Yet, they had a Grandfather of seventy
in the local newspaper yesterday for finding
a copper boiler and he stood in the dock
and claimed that he was going to weigh it in
to help to pay off his last 'Tatting' fine.

The Pissed Misanthropist

He had the Christian name of a Bible Baptist,
was one of the two Tramps living in our Town.
When he was younger he was on his way
to becoming a professional football player
but instead, had some sort of devastating breakdown
and could not seem to ever fight his way back.
The 'Men In White Coats' would lock him up
every few months or so and you wouldn't really
notice the disappearance until he returned.
Then, all of a sudden, there he would be in the park
in the middle of the afternoon on Giro Day
with 10 Regal King Size, a flagon of Strongbow
and a cheap plastic football, drunkenly foot-shuffling.
You rarely heard him talk, Tourette a bit only,
he'd just kick that ball across to any kid passing
hoping that they would kick it back and fore with him.
People always said he was mad (I'm still on the fence
with this one?) for sleeping rough down The Melyn,
what with all the crime, drugs and gang activity
but we all looked out for him, we slapped these two
Port Talbot boys around once when we caught them
hitting him with sticks as he slept on a wooden bench.
I use to find it fascinating to watch him 'hunting'
he would wait a few doors down from the chip shop
for teenagers to come out with their meals open
and steaming salt and vinegar into the Winter air,
then he'd barge straight into them with a "Sorry!"
then walk around the block to return and pick it all up
off the dirty pavement like a King eating venison.
Every Saturday, he'd go up to Woolworths in Town
and take a football out of the basket in the middle
of the shop and start kicking it up and down the aisles.
While they were throwing him out 5 minutes later,
the glue sniffers would be loading up their pockets

with solvents and freezer bags…an unknowing decoy.
I saw him walk into a café on Windsor Road one morning
with a raw half chicken in his hand, no wrapping
just the chicken and beg the owner to cook it, claiming
"I only want the bad half of it you can sell the rest?"
We were all playing the Space Invader machines
after a night of magic mushroom madness and shouting
"Cook the bloody thing for him, mun, c'mon!"
The Park Keeper of Victoria Gardens came up to us
laughing another morning and told us that he'd opened
the Public Toilets at 6am and by 7am they had to call
the Fire Brigade because Matey had staggered in there
drunk and got his cock stuck in the drain grating
in the middle of the floor, he claimed that he was pissing
in the urinal and staggered backwards four steps,
pissing over himself and turned around while falling,
Wham…Stuck…they had to cut him out of there.
I only ever spoke more than two words to him once
and that was the evening before I went to prison
for the first time, I was sat in a warm laundrette
with a girlfriend drinking cider when in he came
out of the rain, he looked cagey at first but then asked
"Who's 'Top of the Pops' this week, then?"
and offered us both a cigarette which we refused
(I remember it well, they were long, thin 'More'
liquorice cigarettes, women used to smoke them!)
I gave him half of one of my flagons of cider
and talk soon turned 'round to prison, he said
"You'll be alright boy, I can tell, just take no shit
off of no one. They've got a TV and a pool table
in the 'Young Offenders Unit' happy days!
The biggest problem you'll have is that you're locked
up 24/7 with other people, it's enough to drive you nuts
if your not nuts already, God forgive me but I hate
other people and the more of them the worse it gets!"
Anyway, I was alright and a few years later I Gypsied

away on my Travels but I was back there a couple
of years ago and he came up in the pub conversation.
Some of the people had clubbed together and bought
him a wooden garden shed and stuck it on the marsh
down by the side of Neath River away from people.
He was happy living there alone for a few months
until Guy Fawkes Night came around and some idiot
school kids went down there and burnt it to the ground
whilst he was drunkenly and peacefully sleeping inside.

The Libertine's Little Black Book

Tumbled out of his sleazy overcoat pocket
one dark, damp Winter's night
and lay there waiting and glowing in mischief.
The next morning a Nun named Chastity
stumbled upon it by the fountain in the market square
where it called out in a throbbing half-silence.
It was wearing an old cracked, fleshy type cover
and as she stooped to pick it up
a dark coldness seeped into her gentle fingertips
and started swarming up both of her arms.
Her once serene head instantly filled to the brim
with crying, screaming and bestial moaning,
whilst nostrils and taste buds flooded and swamped
with alcohol, smoke and many other unfamiliar
shades of foul, unpleasant wickedness.
Her soul started wretching and coming loose
from its fixings until she threw back down the book
to the ground with a 'God Almighty'
and all the Angelic Faith she could muster.
She cringingly shook the darkness back out
from her fingertips as she hurriedly ran away,
leaving the laughing book to await
a less challenging route back home to its Master.

The Azure Lure

For Fourteen long years now
he has watched the changing
Seasons come and go
through a Prison Cell Window.
The Azure Skies of Summer
Torment him the most,
it is then that he feels
his Damned Soul cry inside.
'There is just so much to do
out there, so much to see,
so much to Feel and Experience.
But never for me, no more!
Instead I let a Different
kind of Azure Lure me
into a Violent, Murderous Trap
of Betrayal, Revenge and Cruelty.
All that I Achieved in the End
was to Free Her from Madness
whilst Condemning Myself,
Completely, to a Life Wasted'

Going Nowhere Fast (Life Owes You Nothing!)

To be sat permanently in front of your TV
is really not the best place to be!
Life is really not a spectators sport.
It demands participation and interaction
from the individual involved.
You were given a body that breathes
and a mind that thinks and solves puzzles
(Problems!)
and a short amount of time upon this beautiful,
amazing and magical Earth to enjoy.
All the tools that you need are inside of yourself.
If you do not like a certain aspect of your life
then change it.
If you do not like your life at all
then change all of it.
Sometimes the trick is not in finding exactly
what you should do But in the fact that you are up
and moving and doing something, anything.
Doing boring things will sap your energy
and make your life boring, they should only ever
come into the equation when they involve payment.
Stay in amongst your miserable walls if you want?
Whinging and moaning and as uninteresting
and yawn worthy as a bag of vanilla wallpaper
and you will reap exactly what you have sown.
Yes, you will be proved right in your pessimism,
I promise you that, you are not remotely clever
for it is a self evident and obviously futile road
to have travelled down, the old saying
'Cut off your own nose to spite your face.'
springs to mind.
You can always find a reason to stay in
and not do anything constructive:
'It's raining and I can't be bothered.'

Well, I have news for you: Life can't be bothered
with people who can't be bothered with life.
It's reciprocal.
This sort of thinking is the wrong way around.
You need to be thinking of reasons to be doing
something not avoiding doing something.
So, you did not have a nice time in the past?
So what, welcome to the real world,
you are not special or unique in this at all.
Your Mother didn't love you or not enough,
you were bullied in school, your Ex left you
and on and on and on and on and on...yawn.
That was Yesterday and Today is Today!
Pour all of that crap into some form of artwork
if you are not artistic then join a gym
and take it all out on punch bags
or write it all down on some paper,
have a little ceremony and burn it all.
If you are Spiritual, pray or get smudged.
Do whatever it takes and leave it in the past
once and for all, stop carrying a heavy bag
of other peoples crap around on your shoulders.
I am going to let you into a little secret:
You are only a victim if you choose to be.
Bad things happen to all of us, it's life.
Whoever has hurt you in the past
and in whatever way?
Be happy in the knowledge
that they have gone from your life today.
And if they have not gone, then Leave yourself,
Throw Them Out or call the Police.
It really is that simple!
Or you can sit there and complain
about how complicated it all is
and that it is not as easy as it looks.
Well, Congratulations: you have just Doomed

your foreseeable future to being
both Complicated and Uneasy.
You will make mistakes,
learn from them and then move on.
You will pick the wrong partners,
the quicker that they are gone the better.
You will have negative people around you
who will gossip, backstab and continually
put you down and hammer your self worth.
They are poison, remove them from your life!
Especially if they call themselves 'Family'
There is no Law that states that you have to
speak to anybody even 'Family.'
Remember that Positive family members
support and care while mean, spiteful ones
are your happiness's enemies, get rid of them.
If you are then alone for awhile
then simply be alone for awhile if you have to.
But work to replace them with caring,
supporting and un-judgemental people.
No one is perfect, everyone is flawed.
Forgive yourself your imperfections.
Trust me no one gets through this life unscarred.
Do not always stand directly in the firing line.
Find yourself quiet, safe places to go,
like the beach, the countryside, a mountain,
a sincere friends home.
Take lots of deep breaths and relax, slow down,
re-charge and then get back into the middle
of it, whatever your middle of it might be
and shine harder and brighter each time.
Failure is not an option
whilst Success is within reach
and that is always the case
as long as you are still breathing.
There is no such thing as bad luck.

You did not miss the bus yesterday
because of bad luck
you missed it simply because you missed it,
luck had nothing to do with it,
there will be another one along in 20 minutes.
Whinging, moaning and complaining
merely confuses and clouds life's picture
and dulls our daily work blade.
But unnatural self-doubt is a cancer of the soul.
be always aware of that creeping disease
and nip it in the bud whenever it raises
its un-useful, ugly head.
Remember: Life owes you nothing but Time.
You owe it to yourself to fill up that Time
wisely, constructively and full of goodness.
Spring is in the air, can you not feel it?
I will see you out there somewhere
on this ever changing Battlefield
and Playing field of Life.
You cannot miss me,
I stick out like a sore thumb.
For I am one of the Few
who are Steadily but Surely Winning.

A Strange Day Living Without You Again

Your vein-like roads and streets
partially lit-up at night,
back lanes, subways, bridges, canals
and rough and tumble council estates.
The little 'Big Ben' clock
right next to Victoria Gardens
giving out minutes and hours
to passing solicitors, criminals,
road sweepers and drug dealers
without bias and exactly the same.
That dirty old river
twisting around your belly,
those mountains and hillsides
which shoulder your timeless weight.
Your Market Heart beating loudly
deep inside anyone ever birthed
within your atlased embrace.
The waxing and waning of homesickness,
the magnetic pull towards ancestral bones.
I will never, no more, live there amongst
your hard, calloused finger grips.
Although, I shall carry your fighting spirit
inside my Welsh soul
and your crazy rhythm in my fiery blood
right onto my very last living day.

Dr. Fuckfingers

Wiped the smirk from his cringing mouth,
counted up to 'ten' for composure,
after stopping to laugh insanely at 'five'
for three and a half minutes, silently,
by biting or rather gnawing upon
the left forearm of his white surgical coat,
whilst stamping his right brown comfortable shoe
up and down in a crazed pumping motion.
Until the giddy, euphoric, ecstatic, manic episode
passed and he slid down the wall and onto the floor
in sadness and tears as his mood crashed
completely through the ground around him.
After fleetingly entertaining suicidal thoughts
and only self harming slightly twice,
he finally managed to calm himself with a slap
that his own Mother would have been proud of.
Then after mumbling 'The Serenity Prayer' once
whilst swallowing down four Dexedrine,
he practiced his voice back to normal,
put in place his ordinary, everyday face
and exited the sanctuary of the broom cupboard
bandying about himself nonchalantly
brave and heroic tales of closet spider killing.

Cunt Swagger

There is nothing quite as horny or refreshing
as seeing a beautiful woman
walking down the street and owning it.
It gets nipples and dicks erect, almost instantly.
It's like a breath of fresh air,
a splash of colour across the otherwise grey day.
People start blooming like flowers, bursting
into good humour and cheer, conversations
and warm greetings explode into life around her,
as she tremors the submissive ground,
at heel, beneath her magical and miraculous feet.

The Mermaid And The Rock Pool

The sleepy, fat, porcelain Full Moon
beamed down its silvery smile, shimmeringly
into the darkened, raggedly rocked Cove.
Lighting a match of sapphire and emerald
shading and colour to adorn and glimmer
this salty-fresh, natural, nocturnal palate.
Within this midnight radiance, she sat
waist deep within a canoe-shaped rock pool.
Braiding her hair, thoughtfully, with heart
shaped pieces of Mother-Of-Pearl, whilst
humming softly an almost forgotten shanty.
Pondering the strange rhythm within herself,
she focused then unfocused upon the lullaby
waves lapping at the edges of her concentration.
Deciding at last that what the World needed was
far more Seaweed mixed up nicely in its Poetry.
Her Great Grandmother had a long time ago
given Laverbread and Cockles to the Welsh Folk
to help make them healthy, wise and strong.
Now, she in turn would serenade the deep, sleep
dreams of all sensitive enough to understand
the beautiful dark harmonies of Neptune's songs.

She's Shotting Again

In and out of bovver, razor taxing's and strife.
Back lane traipsing the arse-end of the High Street.
Hoody up, tweaking and on a mission, completely.
Swallowing down another nervous-eyed gulp
of panic and determination.
Fluid and rattling like a regurgitated castanet.
Itching like an abscess and sweating
like the heavy ceiling of a police cell.
She swerves the rubbish binned corner, neurotically
out of the view of CCTV cameras,
up the tooth filling, shaking fire escape
to jaded sanctuary, counting greasy money
down the gang-graffitied, prostitute-ridden hallway.

Your Opinion Gets A 'Fuck Off' From Me, Every Time!

I couldn't give 'Two Fucks'
for how right you think that you are?
This is my life I'm living
and I'm going to do it my own way.
Keep your 'Pinocchio' nose
in your own God Damn business
and your judgemental,
pointing fingers out of mine.
Your opinions mean less than shit!
Curtain-twitching mentality a joke.
Squirm, you envious Bastard, squirm.
I've got a rigid middle-finger for your
lonely journey back to nowhere land.

Celtic

If I were to cut a chunk
out of the side of my Soul
you would see it veined,
marbled and ingrained
completely through
with Celtic knot-work.
Like the age rings
inside of an oak tree
and the candy writing
inside of Porthcawl rock.
I am absolutely riddled
through with Welsh Pride
and Celtic Ancestry,
from top-most leaf
right down to deepest root.

Saving The World And Getting The Girl, Since 1970

I've had my ups and downs like any man
but I'm still here, kicking and screaming
against the insane grain of it all.
Shining like lightning across
the otherwise mundane skies.
Bouncing blasphemously
from one bit of bother to the next.
Always sharpening my teeth
on complicated experience.
That crazy rhythm flowing through my veins
and an 'Outside Of The Box' attitude, always.
The Gypsy, The Traveller, The Rover's friend.
Recklessly knife-edge running
yet in it for the long haul.
At one with Nature, both Human and Countrified.
Cheekily defiant and 'Mastered' by no one.
I refuse to stay still long enough
to keep you company watching the grass grow.
Mapping the seedy midnight back lanes of Soho,
scaling the Abyss of the Soul
and searching for Magic
whilst others fit-in safe, warm and comfortable,
barely aware that their bodies are even breathing.

Old Friend

I was walking through the seaside streets of Looe
when I saw a 'Clairvoyance Today' sign
in a little shop window…so in I went.
She told me many glorious and amazing things
but right in the middle of the reading
she suddenly stopped and said
"You have an Old Friend with you
and he goes with you everywhere.
He crossed over far too young, he's a suicide
and was involved in drugs and just couldn't see
the point in going on any further anymore.
He's laughing and said you had a lot of fun
when you were younger, the mischief and mayhem.
He says to tell you that he 'respects you'
but what he really means and is too proud to say
is that he 'loves you'
He likes where you are living right now
and he likes where you are going.
He loves the night time when you listen
to all of that good music and wishes
he was physically able to drink a beer with you.
He says that there's been a lot of death around you
but you know who and which one he is.
And tonight if you could lift your pint glass
whilst playing music and speak aloud his name
you would make him a very happy man indeed!"

Fuck You Clouds

She was sat upon a broken wooden bench
that I'd seen some Melyn Skinheads
smash a pub payphone upon a few days ago,
three miles in the hills out of Town.
I climbed over the fence stile at the bottom
of the slope that I had just been gathering
magic mushrooms upon and stopped
to light a roll-up around 12ft or so away,
observing her casually as I quickly did this.
She was wearing a railway workers donkey jacket
that looked about two sizes too big for her.
Ripped, bleached jeans and muddy para boots
with a blonde and purple finger length Mohawk.
She had a glass flagon of Strongbow in one hand
and a half-used glue bag dangling in the other
and she was sobbing lightly, tears running
down her dirty yet pretty, young face.
"Are you alright?" I asked as I walked passed.
"Sure, I'm just staring up at the Fuck You Clouds
…please leave me alone and go away!"
And so I did, unexplainably a lot more troubled
than I had been, by miles, a carefree hour before.

Atlas Apathy

She closed her weary eyes
and stuck a pin in a map,
it landed in the middle of the ocean.
She tried again and it struck
a lonesome mountaintop.
"Once more for luck!"
she cackled to herself
nearly choking upon
the unfamiliar sensation of humour.
The pin found home
in the depths of a forest.
She cast both toys of chance
aside with an honest, disheartened sigh
and sat back musing in her emptiness.
I have a Council Flat,
a Chair and a Single Bed,
Portable TV and Radio.
A Gas Fire, 3 Radiators,
Hot & Cold Running Water,
a Toilet and 2 Sinks.
A Cooker, a Hoover, a Microwave
and a Benefits Cheque
every other Monday Morning.
Sometimes it is Wrong
to build up unreachable Hopes.
It's time I Unpacked
my Imaginary Suitcase of Wishes
and Stopped fooling Myself
for I am Not really going Nowhere.

You Bastard, You've Ruined Agnostic Front's 'Something's Gotta Give' Album, For Everyone Now!

I remember arguing with this little, old punk guy
from a small town, somewhere by the coast,
down South, on my travels, a few years ago.
5'2" or there about, lost most of his teeth
(Not through fighting but because his Mother
still brings him bags of jelly sweets around
to visit him twice a week in his late forties!)
I once asked him how he had gotten into Punk,
he had replied that he was picked on in school
so it was an disguise to not be bullied anymore.
And that his Mohawk was also carefully planned,
it was to make him look at least half a foot taller,
oh dear, I had to turn away and bite my lip.
The biggest (or shortest?) coward I've ever met
and I've bumped into quite a few along the road.
Won't fight you like a man, no honour or dignity!
Sympathy and gossip are his only weapons,
clucks like a bitch in a knitting-circle, he does,
behind your back and out of earshot, obviously.
Unless it's on the phone and you're far away,
he called me up one day whilst I was sat reading
Kafka's 'The Castle' and squirmed down the phone
"You Bastard, you've ruined Agnostic Front's
'Something's Gotta Give' album for everyone, now!"
"Prey, explain yourself?" I asked, amused.
"Well, one of the songs on it has your name in it!"
"Oh, I see, well, you'd better take it up with the band,
I'm pretty sure I wasn't in that day, and they wrote it!"
I hung up and tried for the next 15 minutes or so
not to have a hernia from laughing so punk rock hard.

Crazy Rhythm

It's that wired up natural high,
the adrenalin rushing energy.
The dominoes collapsing correctly,
the cue ball smashing the 8 ball
nonsensically yet perfectly.
It's three drinks instead of one,
swaggering in and out of the queue.
Throwing money down-   up.
            -instead of picking it
Tunnel-visioned through the crowd,
untroubled by the emotional weather.
It's smiling at the insane instead of because of it!
The paring sharp the senses,
a cheap day return for a bullet-proof soul.
That crazy rhythm banging
like tribal drums within you
as you gear shift the night under your control.

Roar, You Bastard, Roar!

Though, the Lightning strikes
your furrowed, troubled brow.
Splintering slate fragments
of anger, inwards,
to soar and rage through veins
like coursing, molten dynamite.
Tremor your footwork, steady,
balance the bloody bayonet
of counter-attack with precision.
Unleash with impact and control!
Teeth at work like gears, now,
senses almost a separate creature,
like a Ballerina pirouetting
inside an armoured Tank.
Every part of you is a weapon,
a battering-ram heartbeat
furnacing the violent whole.
Roar, you Bastard, Roar!
and rip right open the seething skies.
No one matters before or after you
for nobody has ever been this so alive.

Burnt Out Blues

Sometimes it is the only sensible thing to do.
When your body cannot take no more punishment,
your brains have been on the ropes for far too long.
You have had loud, fast, screaming, angry music
BLASTING in your poor ears for a month or two,
every knob has been turned up to 11 and broken off!
It is time to hang the mirrors back up on the walls
and give them their proper jobs back again.
Bag the empties in 4 or 5 bin liners, in 2 separate stints
and for Christ Sake, start smoking that cigarette slower.
A gentle walk to the shop to stock up on necessities
electric, gas, sketch pads, porn and comfort foods.
Then it is time to lock the doors and windows,
turn off the phones and slip into your Majestic
Burgundy Bathrobe and jump onto the sleepless settee.
To watch movies, documentaries and daytime TV
for 3 or 4 days in a row, uninterrupted by anyone.
The settee's far more superior to the bed upstairs
at times like these, it's back cwtches you up
without you first having to buy it a couple of drinks
and having to listen to its inane laughter and chatter

Knife, Axe, Sword, Spear (But I'm Still Underdressed!)

Some nights The City is as soothing
and as playfully friendly as a lover,
sometimes as cold and indifferent as an Ex.
Other times it's a barbaric battleground,
where the women in mini skirts and high heels
are merely in disguise, they are really Vikings
on the rampage and you are the only thing
standing in the way of them entering Valhalla.
Every pub is full of Football Hooligans
and never from the Team that you like to watch.
The Police are mob-handed and only waiting
upon eye contact to throw the entire weight
of your Country's Laws down upon you.
Even the Subway Beggar's are aggressive,
with broken Port bottles in their dirty hands
and insults streaming out of their tortured mouths.
It's times like these that you need an escape plan,
time to head back to your local watering hole,
you'll 'read all about it' in tomorrows papers
and be glad that you detoured back to wisdom
and 'learnt the hard way' common sense.

Bowdinnia

There is a land of perfect safety
hidden and waiting not too far away
across the thoughtful footbridge
and through the doorway of daydreams.
There's a sign just outside the walls
which always makes her smile,
it proclaims in big bold letters
WARNING: People Who Like
To Point Their Fingers, Keep Out!
She's been going there since a child
and still does on most week days
when he's in work and the kids
are out of her hair and both in school.
Without it she would simply go spare,
be as mad as a big bucket of frogs.
The charts, maps and geography
keep changing with the rhythms
of her moods, the weather reflects
faithfully her need for peacefulness,
quiet solitude or fun and adventure.
It stretches on forever yet you can
easily walk it in an hour if wanted.
No one knows about her little paradise
for the rot would only follow them in.
She keeps it all locked away safely
deep inside her mind, in that special
corner that she keeps strictly to herself.

Hi, I'm Killing Myself...How Are You?

I walked into The Market Tavern
upon the left hand side of the main drag
at exactly noon on a sunny, Autumnal day.
I spied no one employed behind the bar
but there was a female customer sitting
along the otherwise empty stretch of wood.
I walked on over and stood close by,
glancing sideways at her, late fifties,
un-brushed hair, grey bags under her eyes,
smudged traces of yesterday's make-up.
Also a strange pungent aroma coming
from her which really was quite stunning
in its ferocity and eye-watering thickness.
A mix of stale urine, cheap perfume, grief
(I know this one well, it is unmistakeable!)
rolling tobacco, wet clothing (even though
she appeared dry?) and old library books.
She was drinking a pint of Export lager
and a shot of something whisky coloured.
I was about to ask her where the bartender
was when she turned to me and said
"Hi, I'm killing myself...how are you?"
"Nice to meet you and good luck with that!"
I answered before turning upon my heel
and exiting the building, crossing the street
and strolling into 'The Virgin & The Gypsy'
Where I was greeted by 3 bleach blonde
21 year old smiling barmaids whom I soon
discovered were named Sian, Sam & Billy.
Who served me several pints of Adnams
Broadside Real Ale and a full roast dinner
complete with Yorkshire puddings, pigs
in blankets and all three available meats.
We're all killing ourselves, every waking

moment of our lives, some days are better
and some are worse but right now I was not
in the mood to trade scars with anyone at all.

The Punch And Judy Man

They found him hanging
TODAY!
In the small beach hut
where he kept his equipment.
He was wearing
an Edwardian waistcoat,
a Highwayman's cloak
with his face painted
into that of a sad clown.
There was an empty
litre bottle of vodka,
a handful of barbiturates
and thirteen shillings found
below his dangling feet.
His dolls were propped up
upon a trunk
looking up at Master.
In his breast pocket
was a one worded
suicide note
which simply said
"Goodbye!"

Flash Back

We were on a Y.T.S. (Youth Training Scheme,
for 16 to 18 year olds) called N.A.C.R.O.
(National Association for the Care
and Resettlement of young Offenders)
And on this particular day in question
we were all rounded up into a side room
and given a lecture on the perils of drug abuse.
As soon as the topic of LSD
and Magic Mushrooms came up
I could hear him start to giggle
off to the right of me somewhere
(We'd been in the same gang together
for a few years until his head went,
it was either drugs or the kicking's?)
When they started in on Flash Back's,
he stood up and shouted neurotically
"Fuck off, I don't believe you.
You're saying this to wind me up.
You can't just start tripping on your own,
without taking anything first?"
And with that he walked outside for a smoke.
That was the morning, in the afternoon
we were messing around in the carpentry room
when he banged two hammer heads together,
one of the Supervisors saw it and yelled
"Don't do that, I've seen them explode,
you'll have someone's eye out, you Muppet!"
He went red, then purple, his eyes a mixture
of rage and fear, Paranoia made him its bitch.
"You're mental, hammers exploding,
why are you all fucking with me today, eh?
I've never heard so much bullshit in all my life,
was you having a flash back when you saw that?
You're all in this together, aren't you?

Fucking with my head for no reason at all,
well, you can all fuck off, I'm out of here, losers!"
And he walked out of the building just like that
and started drug dealing in the Town instead.
That is, until a short while later
when he hung himself from a tree up The Gnoll,
only a dog walker stumbled upon him
and saved him the first time, so he went back
the next day to the very same tree and succeeded.
He was alright him, I liked him, a bit weird like
but ain't we all a little strange to some degree?
I once punched him in the face so hard
that he started frothing at the mouth like an dog
and he needed stiches in the back of the head,
we were both aged around thirteen at the time
and it was over gang stuff...I regret that now!

Rum And Resin And The Strumpet Ladder

In a crookedly old midnight tavern
hidden down a dimly lit back lane
upon the seedy harbour side of town.
He slurps the double rum down
from the wooden egg-cup,
the establishment uses as shot vessels,
with a deep growl.
With a strand of straw he lights
by waving it across the tables candle
he ignites his little pipes bowl
stuffed full of Kashmir Black
and Golden Virginia Tobbacy.
He calls the barmaid back on over
with a grimaced wink and orders
another double rum and a tankard
of warm mulled wine and port,
paying with 3 of the 6 battered coins
secreted somewhere in his belt.
He quickly tucks the first one
home to bed and devours half the second
with one greedy gulp.
Hearing a door creaking open up above
and off to the right of him,
he scratches his 6 day stubbled chin
and glances upwards
at female stockinged legs descending
the rickety wooden staircase.
Finishing his drink in a second gulp,
placing his 3 pointed hat
upon his greasy ponytailed head.
He stands up and taking her grubby hand
in his own
he follows her up that Strumpet Ladder.

Strong When Alone

It is a Necessity,
a State of Grace and Mind,
It is the Craftsman's Stage.
It is where the Magic flows
down Mental Rapids of Thought.
Where the Creative Cauldron
bubbles and stews away.
It is the Blank Easel,
the Backdrop,
the Clash with the Gods.
The Purging,
the Shedding,
the Chiselling Away.
The Focus,
the Discipline,
the Siamese Twin
of the Talent.
It Embraces like an Old Lover,
who's both Good and Bad,
it is Darkness and Light
and Everything In Between.
Time alone
is the only way
Through
to the
Power of the Soul
at the Core of Yourself.

Son Of A?

We were sat in a Tavern
deep into the early afternoon,
there was an old western movie
on the TV.
The film finished and Stevie
turned to me and said,

"You know, I don't know if I'm
a son of a bitch, a son of a gun
or the son of a whore, anymore?"

I laughed into my pint,
this is why I liked drinking with Stevie.

"I'm serious man, I'm just lost,
straight up and all the way!"

I laughed into my pint again.

"Hey, I'm starting to get worried,
I'm serious, you know?"

"Yeah, I know Stevie, I'm being serious
too, welcome to the club my friend
and it's your round!"

...And The Bottle Is Empty

The forehead of the bone Full Moon
frowns down big, fat and oppressive,
keeping slightly out of punch range.
As a knot of frustration entangles
my mood giving solitude Chinese burns.
There is a stench of death adrift
upon the crippling Winter wind
yet it is almost certainly not bodily.
The Town Clock behind to the right
neurotically tolls another bleak 2am
as I lift my stiff carcass up off this coffin
smooth park bench and walk unsteadily
in an antisocial fashion across to where
the streetlights adamantly refuse to go.
Then with collar up and jaw fixed
I step onto the dusty old Dram Road
to pilgrim into the night alone just like
my Father and Grandfathers before me